Frances Ellen Lord

# The Roman Pronunciation of Latin

Why we Use it and how we Use it

Frances Ellen Lord

**The Roman Pronunciation of Latin**
*Why we Use it and how we Use it*

ISBN/EAN: 9783337021061

Printed in Europe, USA, Canada, Australia, Japan

Cover: Foto ©Thomas Meinert / pixelio.de

More available books at **www.hansebooks.com**

# THE

# ROMAN PRONUNCIATION OF LATIN

## WHY WE USE IT AND HOW TO USE IT

BY

## FRANCES E. LORD
PROFESSOR OF LATIN IN WELLESLEY COLLEGE

BOSTON, U.S.A.
PUBLISHED BY GINN & COMPANY
1894

The Athenæum Press

Ginn Company

# INTRODUCTION.

THE argument brought against the 'Roman pronunciation' of Latin is twofold : the impossibility of perfect theoretical knowledge, and the difficulty of practical attainment.

If to know the main features of the classic pronunciation of Latin were impossible. then our obvious course would be to refuse the attempt ; to regard the language as in reality dead, and to make no pretence of reading it. This is in fact what the English scholars generally do. But if we may know substantially the sounds of the tongue in which Cicero spoke and Horace sung, shall we give up the delights of the melody and the rhythm and content ourselves with the thought form? Poetry especially does not exist apart from sound ; sense alone will not constitute it, nor even sense and form without sound.

But if it is true that the task of practical acquisition is, if not impossible, extremely difficult, 'the work of a lifetime,' as the objectors say, do the results justify the expenditure of time and labor?

The position of the English-speaking peoples is not the same in this as that of Europeans. Europeans have not the same necessity to urge them to the 'Roman pronunciation.' Their own languages represent the Latin more or less adequately, in vowel sounds, in accent, and even, to some extent, in quantity ; so that with them, all is not lost

if they translate the sounds into their own tongues ; while
with us, nothing is left—sound, accent, quantity, all is gone ;
none of these is reproduced, or even suggested, in English.

We believe a great part of our difficulty, in this country,
lies in the fact that so few of those who study and teach
Latin really know what the ' Roman pronunciation ' is, or
how to use it. Inquiries are constantly being made by
teachers, Why is this so ?    What authority is there for this ?
What reason for that ?

In the hope of giving help to those who desire to know
the Why and the How this little compendium is made ; in
the interest of time-and-labor-saving uniformity, and in the
belief that what cannot be fully known or perfectly acquired
does still not prevent our perceiving, and showing in some
worthy manner and to some satisfactory degree, how, as
well as what, the honey-tongued orators and divine poets
of Rome spoke or sung.

In the following pages free use has been made of the
highest English authorities, of Oxford and Cambridge.
Quotations will be found from Prof. H. A. J. Munro's
pamphlet on " Pronunciation of Latin," and from Prof.
A. J. Ellis' book on "Quantitative Pronunciation of Latin";
also from the pamphlet issued by the Cambridge (Eng.)
Philological Society, on the " Pronunciation of Latin in the
Augustan Period."

In the present compendium the chief points of divergence
from the general American understanding of the ' Roman '
method are in respect of the diphthong **ae** and the consonantal **u**.   In these cases the pronunciation herein recommended for the **ae** is that favored by Roby, Munro, and
Ellis, and adopted by the Cambridge Philological Society ;
for the **v**, or **u** consonant, that advocated by Corssen, A. J.
Ellis, and Robinson Ellis.

# THE ROMAN PRONUNCIATION OF LATIN.

## PART I.

## WHY WE USE IT.

In general, the greater part of our knowledge of the pronunciation of Latin comes from the Latin grammarians, whose authority varies greatly in value; or through incidental statements and expressions of the classic writers themselves; or from monumental inscriptions. Of these three, the first is inferior to the other two in quality, but they in turn are comparatively meagre in quantity.

In the first place, we know (a most important piece of knowledge) that, as a rule, Latin was pronounced as written. This is evident from the fact, among others, that the same exceptions recur, and are mentioned over and over again, in the grammarians, and that so much is made of comparatively, and confessedly, insignificant points. Such, we may be sure, would not have been the case had exceptions been numerous. Then we have the authority of Quintilian — than whom is no higher. He speaks of the subtleties of the grammarians :

[Quint. I. iv. 6.] Interiora velut sacri hujus adeuntibus apparebit multa rerum subtilitas, quae non modo acuere ingenia puerilia sed exercere altissimam quoque eruditionem ac scientiam possit.

And says :

[Id. ib. iv. 7.] An cujuslibet auris est exigere litterarum sonos?

But after citing some of those idiosyncrasies which appear
on the pages of all the grammarians, he finally sums up the
matter in the following significant words:

[Id. ib. vii. 30, 31.]    Indicium autem suum grammaticus interponat
his omnibus ; nam hoc valere plurimum debet.    Ego (note the *ego*)
nisi quod consuetudo obtinuerit sic scribendum quidque judico,
quomodo sonat.    Hic enim est usus litterarum, ut custodiant voces
et velut depositum reddant legentibus, itaque id exprimere debent
quod dicturi sumus.

This is still a characteristic of the Italian language, so
that one may by books, getting the rules from the grammarians, learn to pronounce the language with a good
degree of correctness.

On this point Professor Munro says:

"We see in the first volume of the Corpus Inscr. Latin. a
map, as it were, of the language spread open before us, and
feel sure that change of spelling meant systematical change
of pronunciation: *coira, coera, cura; aiquos, aequos, aecus;
queicumque, quicumque*, etc., etc."

And again:

"We know exactly how Cicero or Quintilian did or could
spell ; we know the syllable on which they placed the accent
of almost every word ; and in almost every case we already
follow them in this.    I have the conviction that in their
best days philological people took vast pains to make the
writing exactly reproduce the sounding; and that if Quintilian or Tacitus spelt a word differently from Cicero or
Livy, he also spoke it so far differently."

Three chief factors are essential to the Latin language,
and each of these must be known with some good degree of
certainty, if we would lay claim to an understanding of
Roman pronunciation.

These are:

(1) Sounds of the letters (vowels, diphthongs, consonants);

(2) Quantity;

(3) Accent.

### SOUNDS OF THE LETTERS.

#### Vowels.

The vowels are five: a, e, i, o, u.

These when uttered alone are always long.

[Pompei. *Comm. ad Donat.* Keil. v. V. p. 101 et al.] Vocales autem quinque sunt: a, e, i, o, u. Istae quinque, quando solae proferuntur, longae sunt semper: quando solas litteras dicis, longae sunt. A sola longa est; e sola longa est.

A is uttered with the mouth widely opened, the tongue suspended and not touching the teeth:

[Ars Gram. Mar. Vict. de orthographia et de metrica ratione, I. vi. 6.] A littera rictu patulo, suspensa neque impressa dentibus lingua, enuntiatur.

E is uttered with the mouth less widely open, and the lips drawn back and inward:

[Id. ib. vi. 7.] E quae sequitur, de represso modice rictu oris, reductisque introrsum labiis, effertur.

I will voice itself with the mouth half closed and the teeth gently pressed by the tongue:

[Id. ib. vi. 8.] I semicluso ore, impressisque sensim lingua dentibus, vocem dabit.

O (long) will give the "tragic sound" through rounded opening, with lips protruded, the tongue pendulous in the roof of the mouth:

[Id. ib. vi. 9.]　O longum autem, protrusis labiis, rictu tereti, lingua arcu oris pendula, sonum tragicum dabit.

**U** is uttered with the lips protruding and approaching each other, like the Greek ου :

[Id. ib. vi. 10.]　**U** litteram quotiens enuntiamus, productis et coeuntibus labris efferemus . . . quam nisi per ου conjunctam Graeci scribere ac pronuntiare non possunt.

Of these five vowels the grammarians say that three (**a, i, u**) do not change their quality with their quantity :

[Pompei. *Comm. ad Donat.* Keil. v. V. p. 101.]　De istis quinque litteris tres sunt, quae sive breves sive longae ejusdemmodi sunt, **a, i, u** : similiter habent sive longae sive breves.

But two (**e, o**) change their quality :

[Id. ib.]　O vero et e non sonant breves.

**E** aliter longa aliter brevis sonat.　Dicit ita Terentianus (hoc dixit) ' Quotienscumque e longam volumus proferri, vicina sit ad i litteram.'　Ipse sonus sic debet sonare, quomodo sonat i littera. Quando dicis *evitat*, vicina debet esse, sic pressa, sic angusta, ut vicina sit ad i litteram.　Quando vis dicere brevem e simpliciter sonat.　O longa sit an brevis.　Si longa est, debet sonus ipse intra palatum sonare, ut si dices *orator*, quasi intra sonat, intra palatum. Si brevis est debet primis labris sonare, quasi extremis labris, ut puta sic dices *obit.*　Habes istam regulam expressam in Terentiano.　Quando vis exprimere quia brevis est, primis labris sonat ; quando exprimis longam, intra palatum sonat.

[Ars Gram. Mar. Vict. de Orthog. et de Metr. Rat., I. vi. 9.]　**O** qui correptum enuntiat, nec magno hiatu labra reserabit, et retrorsum actam linguam tenebit.

It would thus seem that the long **e** of the Latin in its prolongation draws into the **i** sound, somewhat as if **i** were subjoined, as in the English *vein* or Italian *fedele.*

The grammarians speak of the obscure sound of i and u, short and unaccented in the middle of a word ; so that in a number of words i and u were written indifferently, even by classic writers, as *optimus* or *optumus, maximus* or *maxumus*. This is but a simple and natural thing. The same obscurity occurs often in English, as, for instance, in words ending in *able* or *ible*. How easy, for instance, to confuse the sound and spelling in such words as *detestable* and *digestible*.

[Serg. Explan. Art. Donat. Keil. v. II. p. 475.] Hae etiam duae i et u . . . interdum expressum suum sonum non habent : i, ut *vir;* u, ut *optumus*. Non enim possumus dicere *vir* producta i, nec *optumus* producta u ; unde etiam mediae dicuntur. Et hoc in commune patiuntur inter se, et bene dixit Donatus has litteras in quibusdam dictionibus expressum suum sonum non habere. Hae etiam mediae dicuntur, quia quibusdam dictionibus expressum sonum non habent, . . . ut *maxume* pro *maxime*. . . . In quibusdam nominibus non certum exprimunt sonum ; i, ut *vir* modo i opprimitur ; u ut *optumus* modo u perdit sonum.

Priscian says :

[Keil. v. II. p. 465.] Cur per vi scribitur (virum)? Quia omnia nomina a vi syllaba incipientia per vi scribuntur exceptis *bitumine* et *bile*, quando *fel* significat, et illis quae a *bis* adverbio componuntur, ut *biceps, bipatens, bivium*. Cur sonum videtur habere in hac dictione i vocalis u litterae Graecae? Quia omnis dictio a vi syllaba brevi incipiens, d vel t vel m vel r vel x sequentibus, hoc sono pronuntiatur, ut *video, videbam, videbo :* quia in his temporibus vi corripitur, mutavit sonum in u : in praeterito autem perfecto, et in aliis in quibus producitur, naturalem servavit sonum, ut *vidi, videram, vidissem, videro*. Similiter *vitium* mutat sonum, quia corripitur ; *vita* autem non mutat, quia producitur. Similiter *vim* mutat quia corripitur, *vimen* autem non mutat quia producitur. Similiter *vir* et *virgo* mutant, quia corripiuntur : *virus* autem et *vires* non mutant, quia producuntur. *Vix* mutant, quia corripitur : *vixi* non mutant, quia producitur.

Hoc idem plerique solent etiam in illis dictionibus facere, in quibus a fi brevi incipiunt syllabae sequentibus supra dictis consonantibus, ut *fides, perfidus, confiteor, infimus, firmus.* Sunt autem qui non adeo hoc observant, cum de vi nemo fere dubitat.

From this it would seem that in the positions above mentioned vi short — and with some speakers fi short — had an obscure, somewhat thickened, sound, not unlike that heard in the English words *virgin, firm*, a not unnatural obscuration. As Donatus says of it :

[Keil. v. IV. p. 367.] Pingue nescio quid pro naturali sono usurpamus.

Sometimes, apparently, this tendency ran into excess, and the long i was also obscured ; while sometimes the short i was pronounced too distinctly. This vice is commented on by the grammarians, under the name *iotacism :*

[Pompei. *Comm. ad Donat.* Keil. v. V. p. 394.] *Iotacismum* dicunt vitium quod per i litteram vel pinguius vel exilius prolatam fit. Galli pinguius hanc utuntur, ut cum dicunt *ite*, non expresse ipsam proferentes, sed inter e et i pinguiorem sonum nescio quem ponentes. Graeci exilius hanc proferunt, adeo expressioni ejus tenui studentes, ut si dicant *jus*, aliquantulum de priori littera sic proferant, ut videas dissyllabam esse factam. Romanae linguae in hoc erit moderatio, ut exilis ejus sonus sit, ubi ab ea verbum incipit, ut *ite*, aut pinguior, ubi in ea desinit verbum, ut *habui, tenui ;* medium quendam sonum inter e et i habet, ubi in medio sermone est, ut *hominem.* Mihi tamen videtur, quando producta est, plenior vel acutior esse ; quando autem brevis est medium sonum exhibere debet, sicut eadem exempla quae posita sunt possunt declarare.

The grammarians also note the peculiar relation of u to q, as in the following passage :

[Serg. Explan. Art. Donat. Keil. v. IV. p. 475.] U vero hoc accidit proprium, ut interdum nec vocalis nec consonans sit, hoc est ut non sit littera, cum inter **q** et aliquam vocalem ponitur. Nam consonans non potest esse, quia ante se habet alteram consonantem, id est **q**; vocalis esse non potest, quia sequitur illam vocalis, ut *quare, quomodo.*

## Diphthongs.

In Marius Victorinus we find diphthongs thus defined :

[Mar. Vict. Gaisford, I. v. 54.] Duae inter se vocales jugatae ac sub unius vocis enuntiatione prolatae syllabam faciunt natura longam, quam Graeci *diphthongon* vocant, veluti geminae vocis unum sonum, ut **ae, oe, au.**

And more fully in the following paragraph :

[Mar. Vict. Gaisford, I. v. 6.] Sunt longae naturaliter syllabae, cum duae vocales junguntur, quas syllabas Graeci *diphthongos* vocant ; ut **ae, oe, au, eu, ei** : nam illae diphthongi non sunt quae fiunt per vocales loco consonantium positas ; ut **ia, ie, ii, io, iu, va, ve, vi, vo, vu.**

Of these diphthongs **eu** occurs, — except in Greek words, — only in *heus, heu, eheu;* in *seu, ceu, neu.* In *neuter* and *neutiquam* the **e** is probably elided.

Diphthongs ending in **i**, viz., **ei, oi, ui**, occur only in a few interjections and in cases of contraction.

While in pronouncing the diphthong the sound of both vowels was to some extent preserved, there are many indications that (in accordance with the custom of making a vowel before another vowel short) the first vowel of the diphthong was hastened over and the second received the stress. As in modern Greek we find all diphthongs that end in *iota* pronounced as simple **i,** so in Latin there are numerous instances, before and during the classic period, of the use of **e** for **ae** or **oe**, and it is to be noted that in the latest spelling **e** generally prevails.

Munro says :

" In Lucilius's time the rustics said *Cecilius pretor* for *Cae-cilius praetor;* in two Samothracian inscriptions older than B.C. 100 (the sound of **ai** by that time verging to an open **e**), we find *muste piei* and *muste:* in similar inscriptions μύσται *piei*, and *mystae: Paeligni* is reproduced in Strabo by Πελιγνόι : Cicero, Virgil, Festus, and Servius all alike give *caestos* for κεστός : by the first century, perhaps sooner, **e** was very frequently put for **ae** in words like *taeter:* we often find *teter, erumna, mestus, presto* and the like : soon inscriptions and MSS. began pertinaciously to offer **ae** for **ĕ** : *prae-tum, praeces, quaerella, aegestas* and the like, the **ae** represent-ing a short and very open **e** : sometimes it stands for a long **e**, as often in *plaenus*, the liquid before and after making perhaps the **e** more open (σκηνή is always *scaena*): and it is from this form *plaenus* that in Italian, contrary to the usual law of long Latin **e**, we have *pièno* with open **e**. With such pedigree then, and with the genuine Latin **ae** *always* repre-sented in Italian by open **e,** can we hesitate to pronounce the **ae** with this open **e** sound? "

The argument sometimes used, for pronouncing **ae** like **ai**, that in the poets we occasionally find **ai** in the genitive singular of the first declension, appears to have little weight in view of the following explanation :

[Mar. Vict. de Orthog. et de Metr. Rat., I. iii. 38.] **Ae** syllabam quidam more Graecorum per **ai** scribunt, nec illud quidem custodient, quia omnes fere, qui de orthographia aliquid scriptum reliquerunt, prae-cipiunt, nomina femina casu nominativo **a** finita, numero plurali in **ae** exire, ut *Aeliae:* eadem per **a** et **i** scripta numerum singularem ostendere, ut hujus *Aeliai:* inducti a poetis, qui *pictai vestis* scripserunt : et quia Graeci per **i** potissimum hanc syllabam scri-bunt propter exilitatem litterae, η autem propter naturalem pro-ductionem jungere vocali alteri non possunt : *iota* vero, quae est brevis eademque longa, aptior ad hanc structuram visa est : quam potestatem apud nos habet et **i**, quae est longa et brevis. Vos igitur sine controversia ambiguitatis, et pluralem nominativum, et singularem genitivum per **ae** scribite : nam qui non potest dignoscere supra scriptarum vocum numeros et casum, valde est hebes.

Of **oe** Munro says :

" When hateful barbarisms like *coelum, coena, moestus,* are eliminated, **oe** occurs very rarely in Latin : *coepi, poena, moenia, coetus, proelia,* besides archaisms *cocra, moerus,* etc., where **oe**, coming from **oi**, passed into **u.** If we must have a simple sound, I should take the open **e** sound which I have given to **ae** : but I should prefer one like the German **ö.** Their rarity, however, makes the sound of **oe, eu, ui,** of less importance."

Of **au** Munro says :

" Here, too, **au** has a curious analogy with **ae** : The Latin **au** becomes in Italian open **o** : *òro òde :* I would pronounce thus in Latin : *plòstrum, Clòdius, còrus.* Perhaps, too, the fact that *gloria, vittoria* and the common termination *-orio,* have in Italian the open **o,** might show that the corresponding **ō** in Latin was open by coming between two liquids, or before one : compare *plenus* above." " I should prefer," he says, (to represent the Latin **au**,) " the Italian **au**, which gives more of the **u** than our *owl, cow.*"

## CONSONANTS.

**B** has, in general, the same sound as in English

[Mar. Vict. Keil. v. VI. p. 32.] E quibus **b** et **p** litterae . . . dispari inter se oris officio exprimuntur. Nam prima exploso e mediis labiis sono, sequens compresso ore velut introrsum attracto vocis ictu explicatur.

**B** before **s** or **t** is sharpened to **p**: thus *urbs* is pronounced *urps; obtinuit, optinuit.* Some words, indeed, are written either way ; as *obses*, or *opses; obsonium*, or *opsonium; obtingo*, or *optingo;* and Quintilian says it is a question whether the change should be indicated in writing or not :

[Quint. I. vii. 7.] Quaeri solet, in scribendo praepositiones, sonum quem junctae efficiunt an quem separatae, observare conveniat : ut cum dico *obtinuit*, secundam enim **b** litteram ratio poscit, aures magis audiunt **p**.

This change, however, is both so slight and so natural that attention need scarcely be called to it. Indeed if quantity is properly observed, one can hardly go wrong. If, for instance, you attempt, in saying *obtinuit*, to give its normal sound to **b**, you can scarcely avoid making a false quantity (the first syllable too long), while if you observe the quantity (first syllable short) your **b** will change itself to **p**.

. **C** appears to have but one sound, the hard, as in *sceptic :*

[Mar. Vict. Keil. v. VI. p. 32.] **C** etiam et . . . **G** sono proximae, oris molimine nisuque dissentiunt. Nam **c** reducta introrsum lingua hinc atque hinc molares urgens haerentem intra os sonum vocis excludit : **g** vim prioris pari linguae habitu palato suggerens lenius reddit.

Not only do we find no hint in the grammarians of any sound akin to the soft **c** in English, as in *sceptre*, but they all speak of **c** and **k** and **q** as identical, or substantially so, in sound ; and Quintilian expressly states that the sound of **c** is always the same. Speaking of **k** as superfluous, he says :

[Quint. I. vii. 10.] Nam **k** quidem in nullis verbis utendum puto, nisi quae significat, etiam ut sola ponatur. Hoc eo non omisi, quod quidam eam quotiens **a** sequatur necessariam credunt, cum sit **c** littera, quae ad omnes vocales vim suam perferat.

And Priscian declares :

[Keil. v. II. p. 13.] Quamvis in varia figura et vario nomine sint **k** et **q** et **c**, tamen quia unam vim habent tam in metro quam in sono, pro una littera accipi debent.

Without the best of evidence we should hardly believe that words written indifferently with **ae** or **e** after **c** would be so differently pronounced by those using the diphthong and those using the simple vowel, that, to take the instance already given, in the time of Lucilius, the rustic said *Sesilius* for *Kaekilius.* Nor does it seem probable that in different cases the same word would vary so greatly, or that in the numerous compounds where after **c** the **a** weakens to **i** the sound of the **c** was also changed from **k** to **s**, as "*kapio,*" "*insipio*"; "*kado,*" "*insido.*"

Quintilian, noting the changes of fashion in the sounding of the **h**, enumerates, among other instances of excessive use of the aspirate, the words *choronae* (for *coronae*), *chenturiones* (for *centuriones*), *praechones* (for *praecones*), as if the three words were alike in their initial sound.

Alluding to inscriptions (first volume), where we have *pulcher* and *pulcer*, *Gracchis* and *Graccis*, Mr. Munro says : " I do not well see how the aspirate could have been attached to the **c**, if **c** had not a **k** sound, or how in this case **c** before **e** or **i** could have differed from **c** before **a**, **o**, **u**."

Professor Munro also cites an inscription (844 of the " Corpus Inscr.," vol. I.) bearing on the case in another way. In this inscription we have the word *dekembres.* "This," says Mr. Munro, "is one of nearly two hundred short, plebeian, often half-barbarous, very old inscriptions on a collection of ollae. The **k** before **e**, or any letter except **a**, is solecistic, just as in no. 831 is the **c**, instead of **k**, for *calendas.* From this I would infer that, as in the latter

the writer saw no difference between c and **k**, so to the
writer of the former **k** was the same as c before **e**."

Again he says :

" And finally, what is to me most convincing of all, I do
not well understand how in a people of grammarians, when
for seven hundred years, from Ennius to Priscian, the most
distinguished writers were also the most minute philologers,
not one, so far as we know, should have hinted at any difference, if such existed."

As to the peculiar effect of c final in certain particles
to " lengthen " the vowel before it, this c is doubtless the
remnant of the intensive enclitic **ce,** and the so-called
'length' is not in the vowel, but in the more forcible
utterance of the c.    It is true that Priscian says :

[Keil. v. II. p. 34.]    Notandum, quod ante hanc solam mutam
finalem inveniuntur longae vocales, ut *hōc, hāc, sīc, hīc* adverbium.

And Probus speaks of c as often prolonging the vowel
before it.    But Victorinus, more philosophically, attributes
the length to the " double " sound of the consonant :

[Mar. Vict. I. v. 46.]    Consideranda ergo est in his duntaxat pronominibus natura c litterae, quae crassum quodammodo et quasi
geminum sonum reddat, *hic* et *hoc.*

And he adds that you do not get that more emphatic
sound in, for instance, the conjunction *nec.*

Si autem *nec* conjunctionem aspiciamus, licet eadem littera
finitam, diversum tamen sonabit.

And again :

Ut dixi, in pronominibus c littera sonum efficit crassiorem.

Pompeius, commenting upon certain vices of speech, says
that some persons bring out the final c in certain words too
heavily, pronouncing *sic ludit* as *sic cludit;* while others, on

the contrary, touch it so lightly that when the following word begins with c you hear but a single c:

[Keil. v. V. p. 394.] Item litteram c quidam in quibusdam dictionibus non latine ecferunt, sed ita crasse, ut non discernas quid dicant: ut puta siquis dicat *sic ludit*, ita hoc loquitur ut putes eum in secunda parte orationis *cludere* dixisse, non *ludere:* et item si contra dicat illud contrarium putabis. Alii contra ita subtiliter hoc ecferunt, ut cum duo c habeant, desinentis prioris partis orationis et incipientis alterius, sic loquantur quasi uno c utrumque explicent, ut dicunt multi *sic custodit.*

D, in general, is pronounced as in English, except that the tongue should touch the teeth rather than the palate.

[Pompei. *Comm. ad Donat.* Keil. v. VI. p. 32.] D autem et t quibus, ut ita dixerim, vocis vicinitas quaedam est, linguae sublatione ac positione distinguuntur. Nam cum summos atque imos conjunctim dentes suprema sui parte pulsaverit d litteram exprimit. Quotiens autem sublimata partem, qua superis dentibus est origo, contigerit t sonare vocis explicabit.

But when certain words in common use ending in d were followed by words beginning with a consonant, the sound of the d was sharpened to t; and indeed the word was often, especially by the earlier writers, written with t, as, for instance, *set, haut, aput :*

[Mar. Vict. I. iii. 50.] D tamen litteram conservat si sequens verbum incipiat a vocali; ut *haud aliter muros;* et *haud equidem.* At cum verbum a consonante incipit, d perdit, ut *haut dudum,* et *haut multum,* et *haut placitura refert,* et inducit t.

F is pronounced as in English except that it should be brought out more forcibly, with more breath.

[Keil. v. VI. p. 32.] F litteram imum labium superis imprimentibus dentibus, reflexa ad palati fastigium lingua, leni spiramine proferemus.

Marius Victorinus says that **f** was used in Latin words as **ph** in foreign.

Diomedes (of the fourth century) says the same :

[Diom. Keil. v. I. p. 422.] Id hoc scire debemus quod **f** littera tum scribitur cum Latina dictio scribitur, ut *felix.*   Nam si peregrina fuerit, **p** et **h** scribimus, ut *Phoebus, Phaethon.*

And Priscian makes a similar statement :

[Prisc. Keil. v. I. p. 35.] **F** multis modis muta magis ostenditur, cum pro **p** et aspiratione, quae similiter muta est, accipitur.

From the following words of Quintilian we may judge the breathing to have been quite pronounced :

[Quint. XII. x. 29.] Nam et illa quae est sexta nostrarum, paene non humana voce, vel omnino non voce, potius inter discrimina dentium efflanda est, quae etiam cum vocalem proxima accipit quassa quodammodo, utique quotiens aliquam consonantem frangit, ut in hoc ipso *frangit*, multo fit horridior.

**G,** no less than **c,** appears to have had but one sound, the hard, as in the English word *get.*

[Mar. Vict. Keil. v. VI. p. 32.] **C** etiam et **g,** ut supra scriptae, sono proximae, oris molimine nisuque dissentiunt.   Nam **c** reducta introrsum lingua, hinc atque hinc molares urgens, haerentem intra os sonum vocis excludit : **g** vim prioris, pari linguae habitu palato suggerens, lenius reddit.

Diomedes speaks of **g** as a new consonant, whose place had earlier been filled by **c** :

[Keil. v. I. p. 423.] **G** nova est consonans, in cujus locum **c** solebat adponi, sicut hodieque cum Gaium notamus Caesarem, scribimus **C. C.,** ideoque etiam post **b** litteram, id est tertio loco, digesta est, ut apud Graecos γ posita reperitur in eo loco.

Victorinus thus refers to the old custom still in use of writing C and Cn, as initials, in certain names, even where the names were pronounced as with G.

[Mar. Vict. I. iii. 98.] C autem et nomen habuisse g et usum prae-stitisse, quod nunc *Caius* per C, et *Cneius* per Cn, quamvis utrimque syllabae sonus g exprimat, scribuntur.

H has the same sound as in English. The grammarians never regarded it as a consonant, — at least in more than name, — but merely as representing the rough breathing of the Greeks.

Victorinus thus speaks of its nature :

[Keil. v. VI. p. 32.] H quoque inter litteras obviam grammatici tradiderunt, eamque adspirationis notam cunctis vocalibus praefici; ipsi autem consonantes tantum quattuor praeponi, quotiens graecis nominibus latina forma est, persuaserunt, id est c, p, r, t ; ut *chori, Phyllis, rhombos, thymos;* quae profundo spiritu, anhelis faucibus, exploso ore, fundetur.

By the best authorities h was looked upon as a mere mark of aspiration. Victorinus says that Nigidius Figulus so regarded it :

[Mar. Vict. I. iv. 5.] Idem (N. F.) h non esse litteram, sed notam adspirationis tradidit.

There appears to have been the same difference of opinion and usage among the Romans as with us in the matter of sounding the h.

Quintilian says that the fashion changed with the age :

[Quint. I. v. 19, 20, 21.] Cujus quidem ratio mutata cum temporibus est saepius. Parcissime ea veteres usi etiam in vocalibus, cum *oedus vicos*que dicebant, diu deinde servatum ne consonantibus aspirarent, ut in *Graecis* et in *triumpis;* erupit brevi tempore nimius usus, ut *choronae, chenturiones, praechones,* adhuc quibus-dam inscriptionibus maneant, qua de re Catulli nobile epigramma est. Inde durat ad nos usque *vehementer*, et *comprehendere*, et *mihi*, nam *mehe* quoque pro me apud antiquos tragoediarum praecipue scriptores in veteribus libris invenimus.

In the epigram above referred to Catullus thus satirizes the excessive use of the aspirate :

[Catullus lxxxiv.]

> Chommoda dicebat, si quando commoda vellet
> Dicere, et hinsidiás Arrius insidias :
> Et tum mirifice sperabat se esse locutum,
> Cum quantum poterat dixerat hinsidias.
> Credo sic mater, sic Liber avunculus ejus,
> Sic maternus avus dixerat, atque avia.
> Hoc misso in Syriam requierunt omnibus aures ;
> Audibant eadem haec leniter et leviter.
> Nec sibi post illa metuebant talia verba,
> Cum subito adfertur nuntius horribilis,
> Ionios fluctus postquam illuc Arrius isset
> Jam non Ionios esse, sed Hionios.

On the other hand Quintilian seems disposed to smile at the excess of 'culture' which drops its h's, to class this with other affected 'niceties' of speech, and to regard the whole matter as of slight importance :

[Quint. I. vi. 21, 22.] Multum enim litteratus, qui sine aspiratione et producta secunda syllaba salutarit (*avere* est enim), et *calefacere* dixerit potius quam quod dicimus, et *conservavisse;* his adjiciat *face* et *dice* et similia. Recta est haec via, quis negat? sed adjacet mollior et magis trita.

Cicero confesses that he himself changed his practice in regard to the aspirate. He had been accustomed to sound it only with vowels, and to follow the fathers, who never used it with a consonant ; but at length, yielding to the importunity of his ear, he conceded the right of usage to the people, and 'kept his learning to himself.'

[Cic. Or. XLVIII. 160.] Quin ego ipse, cum scirem ita majores locutos esse ut nusquam nisi in vocali aspiratione uterentur, loquebar sic, ut *pulcros, cetegus, triumpos, Kartaginem*, dicerem ; aliquando, idque sero, convicio aurium cum extorta mihi veritas, usum loquendi populo concessi, scientiam mihi reservavi.

Gellius speaks of the ancients as having employed the h merely to add a certain force and life to the word, in imitation of the Attic tongue, and enumerates some of these words. Thus, he says, they said *lachrymas;* thus, *sepulchrum, aheneum, vehemens, inchoare, helvari, hallucinari, honera, honustum.*

[Gellius II. iii.] In his enim verbis omnibus litterae, seu spiritus istius nulla ratio visa est, nisi ut firmitas et vigor vocis, quasi quibusdam nervis additis, intenderetur.

And he tells an interesting anecdote about a manuscript of Vergil :

Sed quoniam *aheni* quoque exemplo usi sumus, venit nobis in memoriam, fidum optatumque, multi nominis Romae, grammaticum ostendisse mihi librum Aeneidos secundum mirandae vetustatis, emptum in Sigillariis XX. aureis, quem ipsius Vergilii fuisse credebat ; in quo duo isti versus cum ita scripti forent :

> "Vestibulum ante ipsum, primoque in limine, Pyrrhus :
> Exultat telis, et luce coruscus aëna."

Additam supra vidimus h litteram, et *ahera* factum. Sic in illo quoque Vergilii versu in optimis libris scriptum invenimus :

> "Aut foliis undam tepidi dispumat aheni."

I consonant has the sound of i in the English word *onion*. The grammarians all express themselves in nearly the same terms as to its character :

[Serg. Explan. in Art. Donat. Keil. v. IV. p. 520.] I et u varias habent potestates : nam sunt aliquando vocales, aliquando consonantes, aliquando mediae. aliquando nihil. aliquando digammae, aliquando duplices. Vocales sunt quando aut singulae positae syllabam faciunt aut aliis consonantibus sociantur, ut *Iris* et *unus* et *Isis* et *urna*. Consonantes autem sunt, cum aliis vocalibus in una syllaba praeponuntur, aut cum ipsae inter se in una syllaba conjunguntur. Nisi enim et prior sit et in una syllaba secum habeat conjunctam vocalem, non erit consonans i vel u. Nam *Iulius* et *Iarbas* cum dicis, i consonans non est, licet praecedat, quia in una syllaba secum non habet conjunctam vocalem, sed in altera consequentem.

The grammarians speak of i consonant as different in sound and effect from the vowel i; and, as they do not say how it differs, we naturally infer the variation to be that which follows in the nature of things from its position and office, as in the kindred Romance languages.

Priscian says :

[Keil. v. II. p. 13.] Sic i et u, quamvis unum nomen et unam habeant figuram tam vocales quam consonantes, tamen, quia diversum sonum et diversam vim habent in metris et in pronuntiatione syllabarum, non sunt in eisdem meo judicio elementis accipiendae, quamvis et Censorino, doctissimo artis grammaticae, idem placuit.

It would seem to be by reason of this twofold nature (vowel and consonant) that i has its ‘lengthening’ power. Probus explains the matter thus :

[Keil. v. IV. p. 220.] Praeterea vim naturamque i litterae vocalis plenissime debemus cognoscere, quod duarum interdum loco consonantium ponatur. Hanc enim ex suo numero vocales duplicem litteram mittunt, ut cetera elementa litterarum singulas duplices mittunt, de quibus suo disputavimus loco. Illa ergo ratione i littera duplicem sonum designat, una quamvis figura sit, si undique fuerit cincta vocalibus, ut *acerrimus Aiax*, et

> “ Aio te, Eacida, Romanos vincere posse.”

Again in the commentaries on Donatus we find :

[Keil. v. IV. p. 421.] Plane sciendum est quod i inter duas posita vocales in una parte orationis pro duabus est consonantibus, ut *Troia*.

Priscian tells us that earlier it was, as we know, the custom to write two i's :

[Keil. v. III. p. 467.] Antiqui solebant duas ii scribere, et alteram priori subjungere, alteram praeponere sequenti, ut *Troiia, Maiia, Aiiax.*

And Quintilian says :

[Quint. I. iv. 11.] Sciat etiam Ciceroni placuisse *aiio Maiiam*que geminata i scribere.

This doubling of the sound of **i**, natural, even unavoidable, between vowels, gives us the consonant effect (as vowel, uniting with the preceding, as consonant, introducing the following, vowel).

**K** has the same sound as in English.

The grammarians generally agree that **k** is a superfluous, or at least unnecessary, letter, its place being filled by **c**. Diomedes says :

[Keil. v. I. pp. 423, 424.] Ex his quibusdam supervacuae videntur **k** et **q**, quod **c** littera harum locum possit implere.

And again :

**K** consonans muta supervacua, qua utimur quando a correpta sequitur, ut *Kalendae, caput, calumniae.*

Its only use is as an initial and sign of certain words, and it is followed by short **a** only.

Victorinus says :

[I. iii. 23.] **K** autem dicitur monophonos, quia nulli vocali jungitur nisi soli **a** brevi : et hoc ita ut ab ea pars orationis incipit, aliter autem non recte scribitur.

Priscian says :

[Keil. v. II. p. 36.] **K** supervacua est, ut supra diximus : quae quamvis scribetur nullam aliam vim habet quam **c**.

And Quintilian speaks of it as a mere sign, but says some think it should be used when a follows, as initial :

[Quint. I. iv. 9.]    Et k, quae et ipsa quorundam nominum nota est.

And :

[Quint. I. vii. 10.]    Nam k quidem in nullis verbis utendum puto nisi quae significat etiam ut sola ponatur.    Hoc eo non omisi quod quidam eam quotiens a sequatur necessariam credunt, cum sit c littera, quae ad omnes vocales vim suam perferat.

This use of k, as an initial, and in certain words, was regarded somewhat in the light of a literary 'fancy.'   Priscian says of it :

[Keil. v. II. p. 12.]    Et k quidem penitus supervacua est ; nulla enim videtur ratio cur a sequente haec scribi debeat : *Carthago* enim et *caput* sive per c sive per k scribantur nullam faciunt nec in sono nec in potestate ejusdem consonantis differentiam.

L is pronounced as in English, only more distinctly and with the tongue more nearly approaching the teeth.   The sound is thus given by Victorinus :

[Keil. v. VI. p. 32.]    Sequetur l, quae validum nescio quid partem palati qua primordium dentibus superis est lingua trudente, diducto ore personabit.

But it varies according to its position in the force and distinctness with which it is uttered.

Pliny and others recognize three degrees of force :

Priscian says :

[Keil. v. II. p. 29.]    L triplicem, ut Plinius videtur, sonum habet : exilem, quando geminatur secundo loco posita, ut *ille, Metellus;* plenum, quando finit nomina vel syllabas, et quando aliquam habet ante se in eadem syllaba consonantem, ut *sol, silva, flavus, clarus;* medium in aliis, ut *lectum, lectus.*

Pompeius, in his commentaries on Donatus, makes nearly the same statement, when treating of '*labdacism*':

[Keil. v. V. p. 394.] *Labdacismum* vitium in eo esse dicunt quod eadem littera vel subtilius, a quibusdam, vel pinguius, ecfertur. Et re vera alterutrum vitium quibusdam gentibus est. Nam ecce Graeci subtiliter hunc sonum ecferunt. Ubi enim dicunt *ille mihi dixit* sic sonat duae ll primae syllabae quasi per unum l sermo ipse consistet. Contra alii sic pronuntiant *ille meum comitatus iter*, et *illum ego per flammas eripui* ut aliquid illic soni etiam consonantis ammiscere videantur, quod pinguissimae prolationis est. Romana lingua emendationem habet in hoc quoque distinctione. Nam alicubi pinguius, alicubi debet exilius, proferri : pinguius cum vel b sequitur, ut in *albo;* vel c, ut in *pulchro;* vel f, ut in *adelfis;* vel g, ut in *alga;* vel m, ut in *pulmone;* vel p, ut in *scalpro:* exilius autem proferenda est ubicumque ab ea verbum incipit ; ut in *lepore, lana, lupo;* vel ubi in eodem verbo et prior syllaba in hac finitur, et sequens ab ea incipit, ut *ille* et *Allia.*

In another place he speaks of the Africans as 'abounding' in this vice, and of their pronouncing *Metellus* and *Catullus; Metelus, Catulus :*

[Keil. v. V. p. 287.] In his etiam agnoscimus gentium vitia ; *labdacismis* scatent Afri, raro est ut aliquis dicat l : per geminum l sic loquuntur Romani, omnes Latini sic loquuntur, *Catullus, Metellus.*

M is pronounced as in English, except before q, where it has a nasal sound, and when final.

[Mar. Vict. Keil. v. VI. p. 32.] M impressis invicem labiis mugitum quendam intra oris specum attractis naribus dabit.

But this 'mooing' sound, in which so many of their words ended, was not altogether pleasing to the Roman ear. Quintilian exclaims against it :

[Quint. XII. x. 31.] Quid quod pleraque nos illa quasi mugiente littera cludimus m, qua nullum Graece verbum cadit.

The offensive sound was therefore gotten rid of, as far as possible, by obscuring the **m** at the end of a word. Priscian speaks of three sounds of **m,** — at the beginning, in the middle, and at the end of a word :

[Prisc. Keil. v. II. p. 29.] **M** obscurum in extremitate dictionum sonat, ut *templum*, apertum in principio, ut *magnus ;* mediocre in mediis, ut *umbra*.

This 'obscuring' led in verse to the cutting off of the final syllable in **m** when the following word began with a vowel, — as Priscian remarks in the same connection :

Finales dictionis subtrahitur **m** in metro plerumque, si a vocali incipit sequens dictio, ut:

"Illum expirantem transfixo pectore flammas."

Yet, he adds, the ancients did not always withdraw the sound :

Vetustissimi tamen non semper eam subtrahebant, Ennius in X Annalium :

"Insigneita fere tum milia militum octo
Duxit delectos bellum tolerare potentes."

The **m** was not, however, entirely ignored. Thus Quintilian says :

[Quint. IX. iv. 40.] Atqui eadem illa littera, quotiens ultima est et vocalem verbi sequentis ita contingit ut in eam transire possit, etiamsi scribitur tamen parum exprimitur, ut *multum ille* et *quantum erat ;* adeo ut paene cujusdam novae litterae sonum reddat. Neque enim eximitur, sed obscuratur, et tantum aliqua inter duas vocales velut nota est, ne ipsae coeant.

It is a significant fact in this connection that **m** is the only one of the liquids (semivowels) that does not allow a long vowel before it. Priscian, mentioning several peculiarities of this semivowel, thus speaks of this one :

[Priscian. Keil. v. II. p. 23.] Nunquam tamen eadem **m** ante se natura longam (vocalem) patitur in eadem syllaba esse, ut *illam, artem, puppim, illum, rem, spem, diem,* cum aliae omnes semivocales hoc habent, ut *Maecenas, Paean, sol, pax, par.*

That the **m** was really sounded we may infer from Pompeius (on Donatus) where, treating of *myotacism,* he calls it the careless pronunciation of **m** between two vowels (at the end of one word and the beginning of another), the running of the words together in such a way that **m** seems to begin the second, rather than to end the first :

[Keil. v. V. p. 287.] Ut si dices *hominem amicum, oratorem optimum.* Non enim videris dicere *hominem amicum,* sed *homine mamicum,* quod est incongruum et inconsonans. Similiter *oratorem optimum* videris *oratore moptimum.*

He also warns against the vice of dropping the **m** altogether. One must neither say *homine mamicum,* nor *homine amicum :*

Plerumque enim aut suspensione pronuntiatur aut exclusione. . . . Nos quid sequi debemus? Quid? per suspensionem tantum modo. Qua ratione? Quia si dixeris per suspensionem *homimem amicum,* et haec vitium vitabis, *myotacismum,* et non cades in aliud vitium, id est in hiatum.

From such passages it would seem that the final syllable ending in **m** is to be lightly and rapidly pronounced, the **m** not to be run over upon the following word.

Some hint of the sound may perhaps be got from the Englishman's pronunciation of such words as Birmingham (Birminghm), Sydenham (Sydenhm), Blenheim (Blenhm).

**N,** except when followed by **f** or **s,** is pronounced as in English, only that it is more dental.

[Mar. Vict. Keil. v. VI. p. 32.] **N** vero, sub convexo palati lingua inhaerente, gemino naris et oris spiritu explicabitur.

Naturally, as with us, it is more emphatic at the beginning and end of words than in the middle (as, *Do not give the tendrils the wrong turn.   Is not the sin condemned?*)

Priscian says :

[Keil. v. II. p. 29.]   **N** quoque plenior in primis sonat, et in ultimis, partibus syllabarum, ut *nomen, stamen;* exilior in mediis, ut *amnis, damnum.*

As in English, before a guttural (**c, g, q, x**), **n** is so affected as to leave its proper sound incomplete (the tongue not touching the roof of the mouth) while it draws the guttural, so to speak, into itself, as in the English words *concord, anger, sinker, relinquish, anxious.*

[Nigidius apud Gell. XIX. xiv. 7.]   Inter litteram **n** et **g** est alia vis, ut in nomine *anguis* et *angaria* et *anchorae* et *increpat* et *incurrit* et *ingenuus.*   In omnibus enim his non verum **n** sed adulterinum ponitur.   Nam **n** non esse lingua indicio est.   Nam si ea littera esset lingua palatum tangeret.

Not only the Greeks, but some of the early Romans, wrote **g,** instead of **n,** in this position, and gave to the letter so used a new name, *agma.*   Priscian says :

[Keil. v. II. p. 29.]   Sequente **g** vel **c,** pro ea (n) **g** scribunt Graeci et quidam tamen vetustissimi auctores Romani euphoniae causa bene hoc facientes, ut *Agchises, agceps, aggulus, aggens,* quod ostendit Varro in *Primo de Origine Linguae Latinae* his verbis : Ut Ion scribit, quinquavicesima est littera, quam vocant "*agma,*" cujus forma nulla est et vox communis est Graecis et Latinis, ut his verbis : *aggulus, aggens, agguilla, iggerunt.*   In ejusmodi Graeci et Accius noster bina **g** scribunt, alii **n** et **g,** quod in hoc veritatem videre facile non est.

This custom did not, however, prevail among the Romans, and Marius Victorinus gives it as his opinion that it is

better to use **n** than **g,** as more correct to the ear, and
avoiding ambiguity (the **gg** being then left for the natural
expression of double **g**).

[Mar. Vict. I. iii. 70.] Familiarior est auribus nostris **n** potius quam
**g**, ut *anceps* et *ancilla* et *anguia* et *angustum* et *anquirit* et *ancora*, et similia, per **n** potius quam per **g** scribite : sicut per duo **g**
quotiens duorum **g** sonum aures exigent, ut *aggerem, suggillat,
suggerendum, suggestum,* et similia.

**N** before **f** or **s** seems to have become a mere nasal,
lengthening the preceding vowel.

Cicero speaks of this as justified by the ear and by custom, rather than by reason :

[Cic. Or. XLVIII.] Quid vero hoc elegantius, quod non fit natura,
sed quodam instituto ? *indoctus* dicimus brevi prima littera, *in-
sanis* producta : *inhumanus* brevi, *infelix* longa : et, ne multis,
quibus in verbis eae primae litterae sunt quae in *sapiente* atque
*felice*, producte dicitur ; in ceteris omnibus breviter : itemque *com-
posuit, consuevit, concrepit, confecit.* Consule veritatem, repre-
hendet ; refer ad aures, probabunt. Quaere, cur? Ita se dicent
juvari. Voluptati autem aurium morigerari debet oratio.

In Donatus we have the same fact stated, with the same
reason :

[Keil. v. IV. p. 442.] Quod magis aurium indicio quam artis ratione
colligimus.

Thus we find numeral abverbs and others ending either
in *iens* or *ies*, as *centiens* or *centies, decies* or *deciens, millies* or
*milliens, quotiens* or *quoties, totiens* or *toties.* Other words, in
like manner, participles and nouns, are written either with
or without the **n** before **s,** as *contunsum* or *contusum, obtunsus*
or *obtusus, thesaurus* or *thensaurus* (the *ens* is regularly represented in Greek by ης); *infans* or *infas, frons* or *fros.* In
late Latin the **n** was frequently dropped in participle endings.

Donatus says that this nasal sound of **n** should be strenu-
ously observed :

[Keil. v. IV. p. 442.] Illud vehementissime observare debemus, ut
*con* et *in* quotiensque post se habent s vel f litteram, videamus
quemadmodum pronuntientur. Plerumque enim non observantes
in barbarismos incurrimus.

**Gn** in the terminations *gnus, gna, gnum,* has, according to
Priscian, the power to lengthen the penultimate vowel.

[Prisc. I.] *Gnus* quoque, vel *gna,* vel *gnum,* terminantia, longam
habent vocalem penultimam ; ut a *regno, regnum ;* a *sto, stag-
num ;* a *bene, benignus ;* a *male, malignus ;* ab *abiete, abiegnus ;
privignus ; Pelignus.*

(Perhaps the liquid sound, as in *cañon.*)

**P** is pronounced as in English.

[Mar. Vict. Keil. v. VI. p. 32.] **E** quibus **b** et **p** litterae . . . dispari inter se oris officio exprimuntur. Nam prima exploso e mediis
labiis sono ; sequens, compresso ore, velut introrsum attracto vocis
ictu, explicatur.

**Q** has the sound of English **q** in the words *quire, quick.*
Priscian says :

[Keil. v. II. p. 12.] **K** enim et **q,** quamvis figura et nomine videantur aliquam habere differentiam, cum **c** tamen eandem, tam in
sono vocum, quam in metro, potestatem continent.

And again :

[Id. ib. p. 36.] De q quoque sufficienter supra tractatum est, quae
nisi eandem vim haberet quam **c.**

Marius Victorinus says :

[Keil. v. VI. p. 5.] Item superfluas quasdam videntur retinere, **x**
et **k** et **q** . . . Pro **k** et **q, c** littera facillime haberetur ; **x** autem
per **c** et **s.**

And again :

[Id. ib. p. 32.] **K** et **q** supervacue numero litterarum inseri doctorum plerique contendunt, scilicet quod **c** littera harum officium possit implere.

The grammarians tell us that **k** and **q** are always found at the beginning of a syllable :

[Prisc. Keil. v. III. p. 111.] **Q** et **k** semper initio syllabarum ponuntur.

They say also that the use of **q** was more free among the earlier Romans, who placed it as initial wherever **u** followed, — as they placed **k** wherever **ă** followed, — but that in the later, established, usage, its presence was conditioned upon a vowel after the **u** in the same syllable:

[Donat. Keil. v. IV. p. 442.] Namque illi **q** praeponebant quotiens **u** sequebatur, ut *quum;* nos vero non possumus **q** praeponere nisi ut **u** sequatur et post ipsam alia vocalis, ut *quoniam.*

Diomedes says :

[Keil. v. I. p. 425.] **Q** consonans muta, ex **c** et **u** litteris composita, supervacua, qua utimur quando **u** et altera vocalis in una syllaba junguntur, ut *Quirinus.*

**R** is trilled, as in Italian or French :

[Mar. Vict. Keil. v. VI. p. 32.] Sequetur **r**, quae, vibratione vocis in palato linguae fastigio, fragorem tremulis ictibus reddit.

(This proper trilling of the **r** is most important.)

**S** seems to have had, almost, if not quite, invariably the sharp sound of the English **s** in *sing, hiss.*

In Greek words written also with **z,** as *Smyrna* (also written *Zmyrna*), it probably had the **z** sound, and possibly in a few Latin words, as *rosa, miser,* but this is not certain.

Marius Victorinus thus sets forth the difference between s and **x** (cs):

[Keil. v. VI. p. 32.]   Dehinc duae supremae, s et **x**, jure junguntur. Nam vicino inter se sonore attracto sibilant rictu, ita tamen si prioris ictus pone dentes excitatus ad medium lenis agitetur, sequentis autem crasso spiritu hispidum sonet, quia per conjunctionem c et s, quarum et locum implet et vim exprimit, ut sensu aurium ducemur, efficitur.

Donatus, according to Pompeius, complains of the Greeks as sounding the s too feebly :

[Keil. v. V. p. 394.]   Item s litteram Graeci exiliter ecferunt adeo ut cum dicunt *jussit* per unum s dicere existimas.

This would indicate that the Romans pronounced the sibilant distinctly, — yet not too emphatically, for Quintilian says, 'the master of his art (of speaking) will not fondly prolong or dally with his s ' :

[Quint. I. xi. 6.]   Ne illas quidem circa s litteram delicias hic magister feret.

**T** is pronounced like the English t pure, except that the tongue should approach the teeth more nearly.

[Pompei. *Comm. ad Donat.* Keil. v. VI. p. 32.]   D autem et t, quibus, ut ita dixerim, vocis vicinitas quaedam est, linguae sublatione ac positione distinguuntur.   Nam cum summos atque imos conjunctim dentes suprema sua parte pulsaverit d litteram exprimit.   Quotiens autem sublimata partem qua superis dentibus est *origo* contigerit, t sonore vocis explicabit.

From the same writer we learn that some pronounced the t too heavily, giving it a 'thick sound ':

[Keil. v. V. p. 394.]   Ecce in littera t aliqui ita pingue nescio quid sonant, ut cum dicunt *etiam* nihil de media syllaba infringant.

By which we understand that the **t** was wrongly uttered with a kind of effort, such as prevented its gliding on to the **i**.

**Th** nearly as in *then*, not as in *thin*.

**U** (consonant) or **V**.

That the letter **u** performed the office of both vowel and consonant all the grammarians agree, and state the fact in nearly the same terms. Priscian says that they (**i** and **u**) seem quite other letters when used as consonants, and that it makes a great difference in which of these ways they are used :

[Keil. v. II. p. 13.] Videntur tamen **i** et **u** cum in consonantes transeunt quantum ad potestatem, quod maximum est in elementis, aliae litterae esse praeter supra dictis ; multum enim interest utrum vocales sint an consonantes.

The grammarians also state that this consonant **u** was represented by the Greek digamma, which the Romans called *vau* also.

Marius Victorinus says :

[I. iii. 44.] Nam littera **u** vocalis est, sicut **a, e, i, o,** sed eadem vicem obtinet consonantis : cujus potestatis notam Graeci habent ϝ, nostri *vau* vocant, et alii *digamma;* ea per se scripta non facit syllabam, anteposita autem vocali facit, ut ϝάμαξα, ϝεκηβόλος et ϝελένη. Nos vero, qui non habemus hujus vocis nomen aut notam, in ejus locum quotiens una vocalis pluresve junctae unam syllabam faciunt, substituimus **u** litteram.

Now it is contended by some that this *digamma*, or *vau*, was merely taken as a symbol, somewhat arbitrarily perhaps, and that it did not indicate a particular sound, but might stand for anything which the Romans chose to represent by it ; and that therefore it gives us no certain indication of what the Latin **u** consonant was.

But we are expressly told that it had the force and sound of the Greek *digamma.*

In Marius Victorinus we find :

[Keil. v. VI. p. 23.] F autem apud Aeolis dumtaxat idem valere quod apud nos *vau* cum pro consonante scribitur, vocarique βαυ et *digamma.*

Priscian explains more fully :

[Keil. v. II. p. 15.] U vero loco consonantis posita eandem prorsus in omnibus vim habuit apud Latinos quam apud Aeolis *digamma.* Unde a plerisque ei nomen hoc datur quod apud Aeolis habuit olim ϝ *digamma*, id est *vau*, ab ipsius voce profectum teste Varrone et Didymo, qui id ei nomen esse ostendunt. Pro quo Caesar hanc ꟻ figuram scribi voluit, quod quamvis illi recte visum est tamen consuetudo antiqua superavit. Adeo autem hoc verum est quod pro Aeolico *digamma* ϝ u ponitur.

What then was the sound of this Aeolic *digamma* or βαυ? Priscian says :

[Keil. v. II. p. 11.] ϝ Aeolicum *digamma*, quod apud antiquissimos Latinorum eandem vim quam apud Aeolis habuit. Eum autem prope sonum quem nunc habet significabat p cum aspiratione, sicut etiam apud veteres Graecos pro φ π et Ⱶ; unde nunc quoque in Graecis nominibus antiquam scripturam servamus, pro φ p et h ponentes, ut *Orpheus, Phaethon.* Postea vero in Latinis verbis placuit pro p et h, f scribi, ut *fama, filius, facio,* loco autem *digamma* u pro consonante, quod cognatione soni videbatur affinis esse *digamma* ea littera.

The Latin u consonant is here distinctly stated to be akin to the Greek *digamma* (ϝ) in sound.

Now the office of the Greek *digamma* was apparently manifold. It stood for ς, β (Eng. v), γ, χ, φ, and for the breathings 'rough' and 'smooth.' Sometimes the sound of the *digamma* is given, we are told, where the character itself

is not written. It is said that in the neighborhood of
Olympia it is to-day pronounced, though not written, between two vowels as $\beta$ (Eng. v). Which of these various
sounds should be given the digamma appears to have been
determined by the law of euphony. It was sometimes written but not sounded (like our h).

The question then is, which of these various sounds of
the digamma is represented by the Latin u consonant, or
does it represent all, or none, of these.

Speaking of f, Priscian says :

[Keil. v. II. p. 35.] Antiqui Romanorum Aeolis sequentes loco
aspirationis eam (f) ponebant, effugientes ipsi quoque aspira-
tionem, et maxime cum consonante recusabant eam proferre in
Latino sermone. Habebat autem haec f littera hunc sonum quem
nunc habet u loco consonantis posita, unde antiqui af pro ab
scribere solebant ; sed quia non potest *vau*, id est *digamma*, in
fine syllabae inveniri, ideo mutata in b. *Sifilum* quoque pro
*sibilum* teste Nonio Marcello *de Doctorum Indagine* dicebant.

And again :

[Prisc. Keil. v. II. p. 15.] In b etiam solet apud Aeolis transire ϝ
*digamma* quotiens ab ρ incipit dictio quae solet aspirari, ut ῥήτωρ,
βρήτωρ dicunt, quod *digamma* nisi vocali praeponi et in principio
syllabae non potest. Ideo autem locum transmutavit, quia b vel
*digamma* post ρ in eadem syllaba pronuntiari non potest. Apud
nos quoque est invenire quod pro u consonante b ponitur, ut
*caelebs*, caelestium vitam ducens, per b scribitur, quod u consonans ante consonantem poni non potest. Sed etiam *Bruges* et
*Belena* antiquissimi dicebant, teste Quintiliano, qui hoc ostendit
in primo *institutionum oratoriarum :* nec mirum, cum b quoque
in u euphoniae causa converti invenimus ; ut *aufero*.

[Quint. I. v. 69.] Frequenter autem praepositiones quoque copu-
latio ista corrumpit ; inde *abstulit, aufugit, amisit,* cum praepo-
sitio sit ab sola.

It is significant here that Cicero speaks of the change from du to b as a contraction.   He says :

[Cic. Or. LXV.]   Quid vero licentius quam quod hominum etiam nomina contrahebant, quo essent aptiora?   Nam ut *duellum*, *bellum ;* et *duis, bis ;* sic *Duellium* eum qui Poenos classe devicit *Bellium* nominaverunt, cum superiores appellati essent semper *Duellii.*

One cannot but feel in reading the numerous passages in the grammarians that treat of the sound of u consonant, that if its sound had been no other than the natural sound of u with consonantal force, they never would have spent so much time and labor in explaining and elucidating it. Why did they not turn it off with the simple explanation which they give to the consonantal i — that of double i? What more natural than to speak of consonant u as "double u " (as we English do w).   But on the contrary they expressly declare it to have a sound distinct and peculiar. Quintilian says that even if the form of the Aeolic *digamma* is rejected by the Romans, yet its force pursues them :

[Quint. XII. x. 29.]   Aeolicae quoque litterae qua *servum cervum*que dicimus. etiamsi forma a nobis repudiata est, vis tamen nos ipsa persequitur.

He gives it as his opinion that it would have been well to have adopted the *vau*, and says that neither by the old way of writing (by uo), nor by the modern way (by uu), is at all produced the sound which we perceive :

[Quint. I. vii. 26.]   Nunc u gemina scribuntur (*servus* et *cervus*) ea ratione quam reddidi : neutro sane modo vox quam sentimus efficitur.   Nec inutiliter Claudius Aeolicam illam ad hos usus litteram adjecerat.

And again still more distinctly :

[Id. ib. iv. 7, 8.]  At grammatici saltem omnes in hanc descendent
rerum tenuitatem, desintne aliquae nobis necessariae literarum,
non cum Graeca scribimus (tum enim ab iisdem duas mutuamur)
sed propriae, in Latinis, ut in his *seruus* et *uulgus* Aeolicum
digammon desideratur.

This need of a new symbol, recognized by authorities like
Cicero and Quintilian, is not an insignificant point in the
argument.

Marius Victorinus says that Cicero adds **u** (consonant) to
the other five consonants that are understood to assimilate
certain other consonants coming before them :

[Mar. Vict. I. iv. 64.]  Sed propriae sunt cognatae (consonantes)
quae simili figuratione oris dicuntur, ut est **b, f, r, m, p,** quibus
Cicero adjicit **u**, non eam quae accipitur pro vocali, sed eam quae
consonantis obtinet vicem, et interposita vocali fit ut aliae quoque
consonantes.

He proceeds to illustrate with the proposition **ob**:

[Id. ib. 67.]  **Ob** autem mutatur in cognatas easdem, ut *offert,*
*officit;* et *ommovet, ommutescit;* et *oppandit, opperitur;* ov-
*vertit, ovvius.*

Let any one, keeping in mind the distinctness with which
the Romans uttered doubled consonants, attempt to pronounce *ovvius* on the theory of consonant **u** like English
(**w**) (!).

By the advocates of the **w** sound of the **v** much stress is
laid upon the fact that the poets occasionally change the
consonant into the vowel **u**, and *vice versa;* as Horace,
Epode VIII. 2 :

“ Nivesque deducunt Jovem, nunc mare nunc siluæ ; ”

Or Lucretius, in II. 232 :

"Propterea quia corpus aquae naturaque tenvis."

Such single instances suggest, indeed, a common origin
in the **u** and **v,** and a poet's license, archaistic perhaps ;
but no more determine the ordinary value of the letter than,
say, in the English poets the rhyming of wĭnd with mĭnd,
or the making a distinct syllable of the *ed* in participle
endings.

Another argument used in support of the **w** sound is
taken from the words of Nigidius Figulus.

He was contending, we are told, that words and names
come into being not by chance, or arbitrarily, but by nature ;
and he takes, among other examples, the words *vos* and *nos,*
*tu* and *ego, tibi* and *mihi :*

[Aul. Gell. X. iv. 4.] *Vos,* inquit, cum dicimus motu quodam oris
conveniente cum ipsius verbi demonstratione utimur, et labias
sensim primores emovemus, ac spiritum atque animam porro
versum et ad eos quibuscum sermonicamur intendimus.    At contra cum dicimus *nos* neque profuso intentoque flatu vocis, neque
projectis labiis pronunciamus ; sed et spiritum et labias quasi intra
nosmetipsos coercemus.    Hoc idem fit et in eo quod dicimus *tu* et
*ego ;* et *tibi* et *mihi.*    Nam sicuti cum adnuimus et abnuimus,
motus quidem ille vel capitis vel oculorum a natura rei quam significabat non abhorret ; ita in his vocibus, quasi gestus quidam
oris et spiritus naturalis est.

But a little careful examination will show that this passage favors the other side rather.

The first part of the description : "labias sensim primores
emovemus," will apply to either sound, *vos* or *wos,* although
better, as will appear upon consulting the mirror, to *vos* than
to *wos ;* but the second : "ac spiritum atque animam porro
versum et ad eos quibuscum sermonicamur intendimus,"

will certainly apply far better to *vos* than to *wos*. In *wos* we get the "projectis labiis" to some extent, although not so marked as in *vos;* but we do not get anything like the same "profuso intentoque flatu vocis" as in *vos*.

The same may be said of the argument drawn from the anecdote related by Cicero in his *de Divinatione :*

[Cic. de Div. XL. 84.] Cum M. Crassus exercitum Brundisii imponeret, quidam in portu caricas Cauno advectas vendens "Cauneas !" clamitabat. Dicamus, si placet, monitum ab eo Crassum *caveret ne iret*, non fuisse periturum si omini paruisset.

Now when we remember that Caunos, whence these particular figs came, was a Greek town ; that the fig-seller was very likely a Greek himself (Brundisium being a Greek port so to speak), but at any rate probably pronounced the name as it was doubtless always heard ; and that **u** in such a connection is at present pronounced like our **f** or **v,** and we know of no time when it was pronounced like our **u,** it is difficult to avoid the conclusion that the fig-seller was crying "Cafneas !" — a sound far more suggestive of *Cave-ne-eas !* than "*Cauneas !*" of *Cawe ne eas !*

But beyond the testimony, direct and indirect, of grammarians and classic writers, an argument against the **w** sound appears in the fact that this sound is not found in Greek (from which the *vau* is borrowed), nor in Italian or kindred Romance languages.

The initial **u** in Italian represents not Latin **u** consonant, but some other letter, as **h,** in *uomo* (for *homo*). On the other hand we find the **v** sound, as *vedova* (from *vidua*), — notice the two **v** sounds, — or the **u** sometimes changed to **b,** as *serbare* from *servare ; bibita* and *bevanda*, both from *bibo*.

In French we find the Latin **u** consonant passing into **f,** as *ovum* into *œuf; novem* into *neuf*.

It seems not improbable that in Cicero's time and later the consonant u represented some variation of sound, that its value varied in the direction of b or f, and possibly, in some Greek words especially, it was more vocalized, as in *vae!* (Greek οὐαί). Yet here it is worthy of note that the corresponding words in Italian are not written with u but with *gu*, as *guai!*

In considering the sound of Latin u consonant we must always keep in mind that the question is one of time, — not, was u ever pronounced as English w ; but, was it so pronounced in the time of Cicero and Virgil. Professor Ellis well says : " Any one who wishes to arrive at a conclusion respecting the Latin consonantal u must learn to pronounce and distinguish readily the four series of sounds : ŭa ŭe ŭi ŭo, wa we wi wo wu, v'a v'e v'i v'o v'u, va ve vi vo vu."

Now the question is : At what point along this line do we find the u consonant of the golden age ?   Roby, though not agreeing with Ellis in rejecting the English w sound, as the representative of that period, declares himself "quite content to think that a labial v was provincially contemporary and in the end generally superseded it."

But 'provincialisms' do not seem sufficient to account for the use of β for u consonant in inscriptions and in writers of the first century.   For instance, *Nerva* and *Severus* in contemporary inscriptions are written both with ου and with β : Νέρονα, Νέρβα ; Σεουῆρος, Σεβῆρος.   And in Plutarch we find numerous instances of β taking the place of ου.

It is true that the instances in which we find β taking the place of ου in the first century, and earlier, are decidedly in the minority, but when we recollect that ου was the original and natural representative of the Latin u, the fact that a

change was made at all is of great weight, and one instance
of β for u would outweigh a dozen instances of the old form,
ou. That the letter should be changed in the Greek, even
when it had not been in the Latin, seems to make it certain
that the 'Greek ear,' at least, had detected a real variation
of sound from the original u, and one that approached, at
least, their β (Eng. v).

Nor, in this connection, should we fail to notice the words
in Latin where u consonant is represented by b, such as
*bubile* from *bovile*, *defervi* and *deferbui* from *deferveo*.

In concluding the argument for the labial v sound of consonantal u, it may be proper to suggest a fact which should
have no weight against a conclusive argument on the other
side, but which might, perhaps, be allowed to turn the scale
nicely balanced. The w sound is not only unfamiliar but
nearly, if not quite, impossible, to the lips of any European
people except the English, and would therefore of necessity
have to be left out of any universally adopted scheme of
Latin pronunciation. Professor Ellis pertinently says : "As
a matter of practical convenience English speakers should
abstain from w in Latin, because no Continental nation can
adopt a sound they cannot pronounce."

X has the same sound as in English.

Marius Victorinus says :

[Keil. v. VI. p. 32.] Dehinc duae supremae s et x jure jungentur,
nam vicino inter se sonore attracto sibilant rictu, ita tamen si
prioris ictus pone dentes excitatus ad medium lenis agitetur ;
sequentis autem crasso spiritu hispidum sonet qui per conjunctionem c et s, quarum et locum implet et vim exprimit, ut sensu
aurium ducamur efficitur.

Again :

[Id. ib. p. 5.] X autem per c et s possemus scribere.

And :

Posteaquam a Graecis ξ, et a nobis **x**, recepta est, abiit et illorum et nostra perplexa ratio, et in primis observatio Nigidii, qui in libris suis **x** littera non est usus, antiquitatem sequens.

**X** suffers a long vowel before it, being composed of the **c** (the only mute that allows a long vowel before it) and the **s**.

**Z** probably had a sound akin to **ds** in English.   After giving the sound of **x** as **cs**, Marius Victorinus goes on to speak of **z** thus :

[Keil. v. VI. p. 5.]   Sic et **z**, si modo latino sermoni necessaria esset, per **d** et **s** litteras faceremus.

## QUANTITY.

A syllable in Latin may consist of from one to six letters, as *a, ab, ars, Mars, stans, stirps.*

In dividing into syllables, a consonant between two vowels belongs to the vowel following it.   When there are two consonants, the first goes with the vowel before, the second with the vowel after, unless the consonants form such a combination as may stand at the beginning of a word (Latin or Greek), that is, as may be uttered with a single impulse, as one letter ; in which case they go, as one, with the vowel following.   An apparent exception is made in the case of compound words.   These are divided into their component parts when these parts remain intact.

On these points Priscian says :

Si antecedens syllaba terminat in consonantem necesse est et sequentem a consonante incipere ; ut *artus, ille, arduus ;* nisi fit compositum : ut *abeo, adeo, pereo.*

Nam in simplicibus dictionibus necesse est **s** et **c** ejusdem esse syllabae, ut *pascua, luscus.*

**M** quoque, vel **p**, vel **t**, in simplicibus dictionibus, si antecedat **s**, ejusdem est syllabae, ut *cosmos, perspirare, testis.*

In semivocalibus similiter sunt praepositivae aliis semivocalibus in eadem syllaba ; ut **m** sequente **n**, ut *Mnesteus, amnis.*

Each letter has its 'time,' or 'times.' Thus a short vowel has the time of one beat (*mora*); a long vowel, of two beats ; a single consonant, of a half beat ; a double consonant, of one beat. Theoretically, therefore, a syllable may have as many as three, or even four, *tempora;* but practically only two are recognized. All over two are disregarded and each syllable is simply counted 'short' (one beat) or 'long' (two beats).

Priscian says :

[Keil. v. II. p. 52.] In longis natura vel positione duo sunt tempora, ut *do, ars;* duo semis, quando post vocalem natura longam una sequitur consonans, ut *sol;* tria, quando post vocalem natura longam duae consonantes sequuntur, vel una duplex, ut *mons, rex.* Tamen in metro necesse est unamquamque syllabam vel unius vel duorum accipi temporum.

## ACCENT.

The grammarians tell us that every syllable has three dimensions, length, breadth and height, or *tenor, spiritus, tempus :*

[Keil. Supp. p. XVIII.] Habet etiam unaquaeque syllaba altitudinem, latitudinem et longitudinem ; altitudinem in tenore ; crassitudinem vel latitudinem, in spiritu ; longitudinem in tempore.

Diomedes says :

[Keil. v. I. p. 430.] Accentus est dictus ab accinendo, quod sit quasi quidam cujusque syllabae cantus.

And Cicero :

[Cic. Or. XVIII.] Ipsa enim natura, quasi modularetur hominem orationem, in omni verbo posuit acutam vocem, nec una plus, nec a postrema syllaba citra tertiam.

The grammarians recognize three accents ; but practically
we need take account of but two, inasmuch as the third is
merely negative.   The syllable having the grave accent is,
as we should say, unaccented.

[Diom. Keil. v. I. p. 430.]   Sunt vero tres, acutus, gravis, et qui ex
duobus constat circumflexus.   Ex his, acutus in correptis semper,
interdum productis syllabis versatur ; inflexus (or ‘circumflexus ’),
in his quae producuntur ; gravis autem per se nunquam consistere
in ullo verbo potest, sed in his in quibus inflexus est, aut acutus
ceteras syllabas obtinet.

The same writer thus gives the place of each accent :

[Keil. v. I. p. 431.]   (Acutus) apud Latinos duo tantum loca tenent,
paenultimum et antepaenultimum ; circumflexus autem, quotlibet
syllabarum sit dictio, non tenebit nisi paenultimum locum.   Omnis
igitur pars orationis hanc rationem pronuntiationis detinet.   Omnis
vox monosyllaba aliquid significans, si brevis est, acuetur, ut *ab*,
*mel, fel;* et, si positione longa fuerit, acutum similiter tenorem
habebit, ut *ars, pars, pix, nix, fax.*   Sin autem longa natura
fuerit, flectetur, ut *lux, spes, flos, sol, mons, fons, lis.*
Omnis vox dissyllaba priorem syllabam aut acuit aut flectit.
Acuit, vel cum brevis est utraque, ut *deus, citus, datur, arat;*
vel cum positione longa est utraque, ut *sollers;* vel alterutra
positione longa dum ne natura longa sit, prior, ut *pontus;* pos-
terior, ut *cohors.*   Si vero prior syllaba natura longa et sequens
brevis fuerit, flectitur prior, ut *luna, Roma.*
In trisyllabis autem et tetrasyllabis et deinceps, secunda ab
ultima semper observanda est.   Haec, si natura longa fuerit, in-
flectitur, ut *Romanus, Cethegus, marinus, Crispinus, amicus,
Sabinus, Quirinus, lectica.*   Si vero eadem paenultima positione
longa fuerit, acuetur, ut *Metellus, Catullus, Marcellus;* ita tamen
si positione longa non ex muta et liquida fuerit.   Nam mutabit
accentum, ut *latebrae, tenebrae.*   Et si novissima natura longa
itemque paenultima, sive natura sive positione longa fuerit, paenultima tantum acuetur, non inflectetur ; sic, natura, ut *Fidenae,*

*Athenae, Thebae, Cymae;* positione, ut *tabellae, fenestrae.* Sin autem media et novissima breves fuerint, prima servabit acutum tenorem, ut *Sergius, Mallius, ascia, fuscina, Julius, Claudius.* Si omnes tres syllabae longae fuerint, media acuetur, ut *Romani, legati, praetores, praedones.*

Priscian thus defines the accents :

[Keil. v. III. p. 519.] Acutus namque accentus ideo inventus est quod acuat sive elevet syllabam ; gravis vero eo quod deprimat aut deponat ; circumflexus ideo quod deprimat et acuat.

Then after giving the place of the accent he notes some disturbing influences, which cause exceptions to the general rule :

[Keil. v. III. pp. 519-521.] Tres quidem res accentuum regulas conturbant ; distinguendi ratio ; pronuntiandi ambiguitas ; atque necessitas. . . .

Ratio namque distinguendi legem accentuum saepe conturbat. Siquis pronuntians dicat *pone* et *ergo*, quod apud Latinos in ultima syllaba nisi discretionis causa accentus poni non potest : ex hoc est quod diximus *pone* et *ergo.* Ideo *pone* dicimus ne putetur verbum esse imperativi modi, hoc est *pōne; ergo* ideo dicimus ne putetur conjunctio rationalis, quod est *ergo.*

Ambiguitas vero pronuntiandi legem accentuum saepe conturbat. Siquis dicat *interealoci*, qui nescit, alteram partem dicat *interea*, alteram *loci*, quod non separatim sed sub uno accentu pronuntiandum est, ne ambiguitatem in sermone faciat.

Necessitas pronuntiationis regulam corrumpit, ut puta siquis dicat in primis *doctus*, addat *que* conjunctionem, dicatque *doctusque*, ecce in pronuntiatione accentum mutavit, cum non in secunda syllaba, sed in prima, accentum habere debuit.

He also states the law that determines the kind of accent to be used :

[Id. ib. p. 521.] Syllaba quae correptam vocalem habet acuto accentu pronuntiatur, ut *páx, fáx, píx, nix, dúx, núx*, quae etiam tali accentu pronuntianda est, quamvis sit longa positione, quia

naturaliter brevis est.  Quae vero naturaliter producta est circumflexo accentu exprimenda est ut, *rês, dôs, spês.*  Dissyllabae vero
quae priorem productam habent et posteriorem correptam, priorem
syllabam circumflectunt, ut *mêta, Crêta.*  Illae vero quae sunt
ambae longae vel prior brevis et ulterior longa acuto accento pro-
nuntiandae sunt, ut *népos, léges, réges.*  Hae vero quae sunt
ambae breves similiter acuto accentu proferuntur, ut *bonus, melos.*
Sed notandum quod si prior sit longa positione non circumflexo,
sed acuto, accentu pronuntianda est, ut *arma, arcus,* quae, quamvis sit longa positione, tamen exprimenda est tali accentu quia
non est naturalis.

Trisyllabae namque et tetrasyllabae sive deinceps, si paenultimam correptam habuerint, antepaenultimam acuto accentu proferunt, ut *Túllius, Hostílius.*  Nam paenultima, si positione longa
fuerit, acuetur, antepaenultima vero gravabitur, ut *Catúllus,
Metéllus.*  Si vero ex muta et liquida longa in versu esse constat, in oratione quoque accentum mutat, ut *latébrae, tenébrae.*
Syllaba vero ultima, si brevis sit et paenultimam naturaliter
longam habuerit ipsam paenultimam circumflectit, ut *Cethêgus,
perôsus.*  Ultima quoque, si naturaliter longa fuerit, paenultimam
acuet, ut *Athénae, Mycénae.*  Ad hanc autem rem arsis et thesis
necessariae.  Nam in unaquaque parte oratione arsis et thesis
sunt, non in ordine syllabarum, sed in pronuntiatione: velut in
hac parte *natura,* ut quando dico *natu* elevatur vox, et est arsis
intus ; quando vero sequitur *ra* vox deponitur, et est thesis deforis.
Quantum autem suspenditur vox per arsin tantum deprimitur per
thesin.  Sed ipsa vox quae per dictiones formatur donec accentus
perficiatur in arsin deputatur, quae autem post accentum sequitur
in thesin.

In the matter of exceptions to the rule that accent does
not fall on the ultimate, we find a somewhat wide divergence
of opinion among the grammarians.  Some of them give
numerous exceptions, particularly in the distinguishing of
parts of speech, as, for instance, between the same word
used as adverb or preposition, as *ánte* and *anté;* or between

the same form as occurring in nouns and verbs, as *réges* and *regés;* and in final syllables contracted or curtailed, as *finit* (for *finivit*).

But since on this point the grammarians do not agree among themselves, either as to number or class of exceptions, or even as to the manner of making them, we may treat this matter as of no great importance (as in English, we please ourselves in saying *pérfect* or *perféct*). And here it may be said that due attention to the quantity will of itself often regulate the accent in doubtful cases ; as when we say *doce*, if we duly shorten the o and lengthen the e the effect will be correct, whether the ear of the grammarian detect accent on the final syllable, or not. For as Quintilian well says :

Nam ut color oculorum indicio, sapor palati, odor narium dinoscitur, ita sonus aurium arbitrio subjectus est.


## PITCH.

But besides the length of the syllable, and the place and quality of the accent, another matter claims attention.

In English all that is required is to know the place of the accent, which is simply distinguished by greater stress of voice. This peculiarity of our language makes it more difficult for us than for other peoples to get the Latin accent, which is one of pitch.

In Latin the acute accent means that on the syllable thus accented you raise the pitch ; the grave indicates merely the lower tone ; the circumflex, that the voice is first raised, then depressed, on the same syllable. To quote again the passage from Priscian :

[Keil. v. III. p. 519.] Acutus namque accentus ideo inventus est quod acuat sive elevet syllabam ; gravis vero eo quod deprimat aut deponet ; circumflexus ideo quod deprimat et acuat.

In conclusion of this part of the work the following anecdotes from Aulus Gellius are given, as serving to show that to the rules of classic Roman pronunciation there were exceptions, apparently more or less arbitrary, some — perhaps many — of which we may not now hope to discover; and as serving still more usefully to show, by the stress laid upon points of comparative insignificance, that exceptions were rare, such as even scholars could afford to disagree upon, and not such as to affect the general tenor of the language. So that we are encouraged to believe that, as the English language may be well and even elegantly spoken by those whose speech still includes scores, if not hundreds, of variations in pronunciation, in sounds of letters or in accent, so we may hope to pronounce the Latin with some good degree of satisfaction, whether, for instance, we say *quiésco* or *quiésco, ăctito* or *āctito :*

[Aul. Gell. VI. xv.] Amicus noster, homo multi studii atque in bonarum disciplinarum opere frequens, verbum *quiescit* usitate e littera correpta dixit. Alter item amicus homo in doctrinis, quasi in praestigiis, mirificus, communiumque vocum respuens nimis et fastidiens, barbare eum dixisse opinatus est; quoniam producere debuisset, non corripere. Nam *quiescit* ita oportere dici praedicavit, ut *calescit, nitescit, stupescit,* atque alia hujuscemodi multa. Id etiam addebat, quod *quies* e producto, non brevi, diceretur. Noster autem, qua est omnium rerum verecunda mediocritate, ne si Aelii quidem Cincii et Santrae dicendum ita censuissent obsecuturum sese fuisse ait, contra perpetuam Latinae linguae consuetudinem. Neque se tam insignite locuturum, absona aut inaudita ut diceret. Litteras autem super hac re fecit, item inter haec exercitia quaedam ludicra; et *quiesco* non esse his simile quae supra posui, nec a *quiete* dictum, sed ab eo *quietem;* Graecaeque vocis ἴσχον καὶ ἔσκον, Ionice a verbo ἴσχω ἴσχω, et modum et originem verbum illud habere demonstravit. Rationibusque haud sane frigidis docuit *quiesco* e littera longa dici non convenire.

[Aul. Gell. IX. vi.]   Ab eo, quod est *ago* et *egi*, verba sunt quae
appellant grammatici frequentativa, *actito* et *actitavi*.   Haec
quosdam non sane indoctos viros audio ita pronuntiare ut primam
in his litteram corripiant ; rationemque dicant, quoniam in verbo
principali, quod est *ago*, prima littera breviter pronuntiatur.   Cur
igitur ab eo quod est *edo* et *ungo*, in quibus verbis prima littera
breviter dicitur, *esito* et *unctito*, quae sunt eorum frequentativa
prima littera longa promimus? et contra, *dictito*, ab eo verbo
quod est *dico*, correpte dicimus?   Num ergo potius *actito* et
*actitavi* producenda sunt? quoniam frequentativa ferme omnia
eodem modo in prima syllaba dicuntur, quo participia praeteriti
temporis ex iis verbis unde ea profecta sunt in eadem syllaba pro-
nuntiantur ; sicut *lego, lectus, lectito* facit ; *ungo, unctus, unctito ;
scribo, scriptus, scriptito ; moneo, monitus, monito ; pendeo, pen-
sus, pensito ; edo, esus, esito ; dico,* autem, *dictus, dictito* facit ;
*gero, gestus, gestito ; veho, vectus, vectito ; rapio, raptus, raptito ;
capio, captus, captito ; facio, factus, factito.*   Sic igitur *actito*
producte in prima syllaba pronuntiandum, quoniam ex eo fit quod
est *ago* et *actus.*

## PART II.

## HOW TO USE IT.

THE directions now to be given may be fittingly introduced by a few paragraphs from Professor Munro's pamphlet on the pronunciation of Latin, already more than once quoted from.   He says — and part of this has been cited before :

"We know exactly how Cicero or Quintilian did or could spell ; we know the syllable on which they placed the accent of almost every word ; and in almost every case we already follow them in this.   I have the conviction that in their best days philological people took vast pains to make the writing exactly reproduce the sounding; and that if Quintilian or Tacitus spelt a word differently from Cicero or Livy, he also spoke it so far differently.   With the same amount of evidence, direct and indirect, we have for Latin, it would not, I think, be worth anybody's while to try to recover the pronunciation of French or English; it might, I think, be worth his while to try to recover that of German or Italian, in which sound and spelling accord more nearly, and accent obeys more determinable laws."

" I am convinced," he says in another place, " that the mainstay of an efficient reform is the adoption essentially of the Italian vowel system : it combines beauty, firmness and precision in a degree not equalled by any other system of which I have any knowledge.   The little ragged boys in the streets of Rome and Florence enunciate their vowels in a style of which princes might be proud."

And again :

" I do not propose that every one should learn Italian in order to learn Latin. What I would suggest is, that those who know Italian should make use of their knowledge and should in many points take Italian sounds for the model to be followed ; that those who do not know it should try to learn from others the sounds required, or such an approximation to them as may be possible in each case."

We may then sum up the results at which we have arrived in the following directions :

First of all pay particular attention to the vowel sounds, to make them full and distinct, taking the Italian model, if you know Italian, and always observing strictly the quantity.

Pronounce

ā as in Italian *fato;* or as final a in aha !

ă as in Italian *fatto;* or as initial a in aha ! or as in fast (not as in fat).

ē as second e in Italian *fedele;* or as in fête (not fate) ; or as in vein.

ĕ as in Italian *fetta;* or as in very.

ī as first i in Italian *timide;* or as in caprice.

ĭ as second i in Italian *timide;* or as in capricious.

ĭ or ŭ, where the spelling varies between the two (e.g. *maximus, maxumus*), as in German Müller.

ō as first o in Italian *orlo;* or as in more.

ŏ as first o in Italian *rotto;* or as in wholly (not as in holly).

ū as in Italian *rumore;* or as in rural.

ŭ as in Italian *ruppe;* or as in puss (not as in fuss).

Let i in vĭ before d, t, m, r or x, in the first syllable of a word, be pronounced quite obscurely, somewhat as first i in virgin.

In the matter of diphthongs, be sure to take always the correct spelling, to begin with, and thus avoid what Munro

justly terms "hateful barbarisms like *coelum, coena, moestus*."
Much time is wasted by students and bad habits are acquired
in not finding, at the outset, the right spelling of each word
and holding to it.   This each student must do for himself,
consulting a good dictionary, as editors and editions are not
always to be depended on.   Here it is the diphthongs that
present the chief difficulty and call for the greatest care.

In pronouncing diphthongs sound both vowels, but glide
so rapidly from the first to the second as to offer to the ear
but a single sound.   In the publication of the Cambridge
(Eng.) Philological Society on "Pronunciation of Latin in
the Augustan Period," the following directions are given:

"The pronunciation of these diphthongs, of which the
last three are extremely rare, is best learnt by first sounding
each vowel separately and then running them together, **ae**
as ah-eh, **au** as ah-oo, **oe** as o-eh, **ei** as eh-ee, **eu** as eh-oo,
and **ui** as oo-ee."

Thus :

> **ae** (ah-éh) as in German *näher;* or as **ea** in pear ; or **ay** in
> aye (ever); (not like ā in fate nor like **ai** in aisle).
>
> **ai** (ah-ée) as in aye (yes).
>
> **au** (ah-óo) as in German *Haus*, with more of the **u** sound than
> **ou** in house.
>
> **ei** (eh-ée) nearly as in veil.   (In *dein, deinde*, the **ei** is not a
> diphthong, but the **e**, when not forming a distinct syllable,
> is elided.)
>
> **eu** (eh-óo) as in Italian *Europa*.   (In *neuter* and *neutiquam*
> elide the **e**.)
>
> **oe** (o-éh) nearly like German ö in *Goethe*.
>
> **oi** is not found in the classical period.   (In *proin, proinde*, the
> **o** is either elided or forms a distinct syllable.   **ou** in *prout*
> is not a diphthong ; the **u** is either elided or forms a dis-
> tinct syllable.)
>
> **ui** (oo-ée) as in cuirass.

In the pronunciation of consonants certain points claim
special attention. And first among these is the sounding of
the doubled consonants. Whoever has heard Italian spoken
recognizes one of its greatest beauties to be the distinctness,
yet smoothness, with which its ll and rr and cc — in short, all
its doubled consonants — are pronounced. No feature of
the language is more charming. And one who attempts the
same in Latin and perseveres, with whatever difficulty and
pains, will be amply rewarded in the music of the language.

A good working rule for pronouncing doubled consonants
is to hold the first until ready to pronounce the second : as
in the words *we'll lie till late*, not to be pronounced as *we lie
till eight*.

Next in importance, and, in New England at least, first in
difficulty, is the trilling of the r. There can be no approximation to a satisfactory pronunciation of Latin until this r
is acquired ; but the satisfaction in the result when accom-
plished is well worth all the pains taken.

Another point to be observed is that the dentals t, d, n, l,
require that the tongue touch the teeth, rather than the
palate. Munro says : "d and t we treat with our usual
slovenliness, and force them up to the roof of our mouth :
we should make them real dentals, as no doubt the Romans
made them, and then we shall see how readily *ad at, apud
aput, illud illut* and the like interchange." This requires
care, but amply repays the effort.

It is necessary also to remember that n before a guttural
is pronounced as in the same position in English, e.g., in
*ancora* as in anchor ; in *anxius* as in anxious ; in *relinquo* as
in relinquish.

Remember to make n before f or s a mere nasal, having
as little prominence otherwise as possible, and to carefully
lengthen the preceding vowel.

Studiously observe the length of the vowel before the terminations *gnus, gna, gnum.*

Remember that the final syllable in **m**, when not elided, is to be pronounced as lightly and rapidly as possible, the more lightly and indistinctly the better.

Remember that **s** must not be pronounced as **z**, except where it represents **z** in Greek words, as Smyrna (Zmyrna), Smaragdus (Zmaragdus), otherwise always pronounce as in sis.

Remember in pronouncing **v** to direct the lower lip toward the upper lip, avoiding the upper teeth.

In general, in pronouncing the consonants conform to the following scheme :

**b** as in blab.

**b** before **s** or **t**, sharpened to **p**, as *urbs = urps; obtinuit = optinuit.*

**c** as sceptic (never as in sceptre).

**ch** as in chemist (never as in cheer or chivalry).

**d** as in did, but made more dental than in English.

**d** final, before a word beginning with a consonant, in particles especially, often sharpened to **t** as in tid-bit (tit-bit).

**f** as in fief, but with more breath than in English.

**g** as in gig (never as in gin).

**gn** in terminations *gnus, gna, gnum*, makes preceding vowel long.

**h** as in hah !

**i** (consonant) as in onion.

**k** as in kink.

**l** initial and final, as in lull.

**l** medial, as in lullaby, always more dental than in English.

**m** initial and medial, as in membrane.

**m** before **q**, nasalized.

**m** final, when not elided, touched lightly and obscurely, somewhat as in tandem (tandm) ; or as in the Englishman's pronunciation of Blenheim (Blenhm), Birmingham (Birminghm).

n initial and final, as in nine.

n medial, as in damnable, always more dental than in English.

n before c, g, q, x, as in concord, anger, sinker, relinquish, anxious, the tongue not touching the roof of the mouth.

n before f or s, nasal, lengthening the preceding vowel, as in *renaissance.*

p as in pup.

q as in quick.

r as in roar, but trilled, as in Italian or French. (This is most important.)

s as in sis (never as in his).

t as in tot, but more dental than in English (never as in motion).

th nearly as in then (never as in thin).

v (u consonant) nearly as in verve, but labial, rather than labio-dental; like the German w (not like the English w). Make English v as nearly as may be done without touch- the lower lip to the upper teeth.

x as in six.

z nearly as dz in adze.

Doubled consonants to be pronounced each distinctly, by holding the first until ready to pronounce the second.

As Professor Ellis well puts it : "No relaxation of the organs, no puff of wind or grunt of voice should intervene between the two parts of a doubled consonant, which should more resemble separated parts of one articulation than two separate articulations."

"Duplication of consonants is consequently regarded simply as the energetic utterance of a single consonant."

### ELISION.

Professor Ellis believes that the m was always omitted in speaking and the following consonant pronounced as if doubled (*quorum pars* as *quoruppars*). Final m at the end of a sentence he thinks was not heard at all. Where a vowel followed he thinks that the **m** was not heard, the vowel before being slurred on to the initial vowel of the following word.

The Cambridge (Eng.) Philological Society, however, takes the view that "final vowels (or diphthongs) when followed by vowels (or diphthongs) were not cut off, but lightly run on to the following word, as in Italian. But if the vowel was the same the effect was that of a single sound."

Professor Munro says :

"In respect of elision I would only say that, by comparing Plautus with Ovid, we may see how much the elaborate cultivation of the language had tended to a more distinct sounding of final syllables ; and that but for Virgil's powerful influence the elision of long vowels would have almost ceased. Clearly we must not altogether pass over the elided vowel or syllable in **m**, except perhaps in the case of ĕ in common words, *que, neque,* and the like."

This view, held by the Cambridge Philological Society and by Professor Munro, is the one generally accepted ; the practice recommended by them is the one generally in use, and that which seems safe and suitable to follow. That is : Do not altogether pass over the elided vowel or syllable in **m**, except in cases of very close connection, in compound words or phrases, or when the final and initial vowel are the same, or in the case of ĕ final in common words, as *que, neque,* and the like ; but let the final vowel run lightly on to the following vowel as in Italian, and touch lightly and obscurely the final syllable in **m**. The **o** or **e** of *proin, proinde, prout, dein, deinde, neuter, neutiquam,* when not forming a distinct syllable, are to be treated as cases of elision between two words.

## QUANTITY.

In the pronunciation of Latin the observance of quantity and of pitch are the two most difficult points of attainment; and they are the crucial test of good reading.

The observance of quantity is no less important in prose than in verse. A little reflection will convince the dullest mind that the Romans did not pronounce a word one way in prose and another in verse, that we have not in poetry and prose two languages. Cicero and Quintilian both enjoin a due admixture of long and short syllables in prose as well as verse; and any one who takes delight in reading Latin will heartily agree with Professor Munro when he says: "For myself, by observing quantity, I seem to feel more keenly the beauty of Cicero's style and Livy's, as well as Virgil's and Horace's."

Therefore until one feels at home with the quantities, let him observe the rule of beating time in reading, to make sure that the long syllables get twice the time of the short ones. In this way he will soon have the pronunciation of each word correctly fixed in mind, and will not be obliged to think of his quantities in verse more than in prose. A long step has been taken in the enjoyment of Latin poetry when the reader does not have to be thinking of the 'feet.'

Young students particularly should be especially careful in the final syllable of the verse. Since, so far as the measure is concerned, there is no difference there between the long and the short syllable, the reader is apt to be careless as to the length of the syllable itself, and to make all final syllables long, even to the mispronouncing of the word, thereby both making a false quantity and otherwise injuring the effect of the verse, by importing into it a monotony foreign to the original. Does not Cicero himself say that a short syllable at the end of the verse is as if you 'stood (came to a stand), but a long one as if you 'sat down'?

It is, in fact, in the pronouncing of final syllables everywhere that the most serious and persistent faults are found, *būs* for *bŭs* being one of the worst and most common cases. How much of the teacher's time might be spared, for better things, if he did not have to correct *būs* into *bŭs* !

The disposition to neglect the double and doubled consonants is another serious fault, as well as the slovenly pronunciation of two consonants, where the reader fails to give the time necessary to speak each distinctly, making false quantity and mispronunciation at the same time.

In general, if two symbols are written we are to infer that two sounds were intended. The only exception to this is in the case of a few words where the spelling varies, as *casso* or *caso*. In such cases we may suppose that the doubled consonant was only designed to indicate length.

Another, apparent, exception is in the case of a mute followed by a liquid ; but the mute and liquid are regularly sounded as one, and therefore do not affect the length of the preceding vowel. Sometimes, however, for the sake of time, the verse requires them to be pronounced separately. In this case each is to be given distinctly ; the mute and liquid must not coalesce. For it must not be forgotten that, as a rule, the vowel before a mute followed by a liquid is short, in which case it must on no account be lengthened. Thus, ordinarily, we say *pă-tris*, but the verse may require *pat-ris*.

Although the vowel before two consonants is generally short, we find, in some instances, a long vowel in this position. For example, it would appear that the vowel of the supine and cognate parts of the verb is long if the vowel of the present indicative, though short, is followed by a medial (**b, g, d, z**), as *āctus*, *lēctus*, from *ăgo*, *lĕgo*.

Let it be remembered in the matter of **i** consonant between two vowels, that we have really the force of two **ii**'s, as originally written, one, vowel, making a diphthong with the preceding, the other, consonant, introducing the new syllable ; and that the same is true of the compounds of *jacio*, which should be written with a single **i** but pronounced as with two, as *obicit (objicit)*.

### ACCENT.

The question of accent presents little difficulty as to place, but some as to quality, and much as to kind.

As to quality, it must be remembered that while the acute accent is found on syllables either short or long (by nature or position), and on either the penult or the antepenult, the circumflex is found only on long vowels, and (in words of more than one syllable) only on the penult, and then only in case the ultima is short.  Thus, *spés*, but *dúx; lúnă*, but *lúnā; legâtus*, but *legáti*.  In these examples the length of the syllable is the same and of course remains the same in inflection, but the quality of the accent changes.  In the one case the voice is both raised and depressed on the same syllable, in the other it is only raised.  As Professor Ellis puts it : " If the last syllable but one is long, it is spoken with a raised pitch, which is maintained throughout if its vowel is short, as : *véntōs*, or if the last syllable is long, as : *fāmāe;* but sinks immediately if its own vowel is long, and at the same time the vowel of the last syllable is short, as *fámă*, to be distinguished from *fămā*."

But when we come to the question of the *kind* of accent, we come upon the most serious matter practically in the pronunciation of Latin, and this because of a difficulty peculiar to the English speaking peoples.  The English accent is one of *stress*, whereas the Roman is one of *pitch*.

No one will disagree with Professor Ellis when he "assumes," in his Quantitative Pronunciation of Latin, "that the Augustan Romans had *no* force accent, that is, that they did not, as we do, distinguish one syllable in every word *invariably* by pronouncing it with greater force, that is, with greater loudness, than the others, but that the force varied according to the feeling of the moment, or the beat of the timekeeper in singing, and was used for purposes of expression ; just as with us, musical pitch is free, that is, just as we may pronounce the same word with different musical pitches for its different syllables, and in fact are obliged to vary the musical pitch in interrogations and replies. The fixity of musical pitch and freedom of degrees of force in Latin, and the freedom of musical pitch and fixity of degrees of force in English sharply distinguish the two pronunciations even irrespective of quantity."

But this pitch accent, while alien to us, is not impossible of acquisition, and it is essential to any adequate rendering of any Latin writer, whether of prose or verse. Nor will the attainment be a work of indefinite time if one pursues with constancy some such course as the following, recommended by Professor Ellis :

"The place of raised pitch," he says, "must be strictly observed, and for this purpose the verses had better be first read in a kind of sing-song, the high pitched syllables being all of one pitch and the low pitched syllables being all of one pitch also, but about a musical 'fifth' lower than the other, as if the latter were sung to the lowest note of the fourth string of a violin, and the former were sung to the lowest note of its third string."

In the foregoing pages an effort has been made to bring together compactly and to set forth concisely the nature of the 'Roman method' of pronouncing Latin; the reasons for adopting, and the simplest means of acquiring it. No attempt has been made at a philosophical or exhaustive treatment of the subject; but at the same time it is hoped that nothing unphilosophical has crept in, or anything been omitted, which might have been given, to render the subject intelligible and enable the intelligent reader to understand the points and be able to give a reason for each usage herein recommended.

The main object in view in preparing this little book has been to help the teachers of Latin in the secondary schools, to furnish them something not too voluminous, yet as satisfactory as the nature of the case allows, upon a subject which the present diversity of opinion and practice has rendered unnecessarily obscure.

To these teachers, then, a word from Professor Ellis may be fitly spoken in conclusion :

"To teach a person to read prose *well*, even in his own language, is difficult, partly because he has seldom heard prose well read, though he is constantly hearing prose around him, intonated, but unrhythmical. In the case of a dead language, like the Latin, which the pupil never hears spoken, and seldom hears read, except by himself or his equally ignorant and hobbling fellow-scholars, this difficulty is inordinately increased. Let me once more impress on every teacher of Latin the *duty* of himself learning to read Latin readily according to accent and quantity ; the *duty* of his reading out to his pupils, of his setting them a *pattern*, of his hearing that they follow it, of his correcting their mistakes, of his *leading* them into right habits. If the quantitative pronunciation be adopted, no one will be fit to become a classical teacher who cannot read a simple Latin sentence decently, with a strict observance of that quantity by which alone the greatest of Latin orators regulated his own rhythms."

"All pronunciation is acquired by imitation, and it is not till after hearing a sound many times that we are able to grasp it sufficiently well to imitate. It is a mistake constantly made by teachers of language to suppose that a pupil knows by once hearing unfamiliar sounds, or even unfamiliar combinations of familiar sounds. When pupils are made to imitate too soon, they acquire an erroneous pronunciation, which they afterward hear constantly from themselves actually or mentally, and believe that they hear from the teacher during the small fraction of a second that each sound lasts, and hence the habits of these organs become fixed."

The following direction is of the utmost importance (Curwen's "Standard Course," p. 3) : "The teacher never sings (speaks) *with* his pupils, but sings (utters, reads, dictates) to them a brief and soft *pattern*. The first art of the pupil is to *listen well* to the pattern, and then to imitate it exactly. He that listens best sings (speaks) best."